Borough of Twickenham
Local Hist

Paper Nur

WHEN THE BOMBS FELL

Twickenham, Teddington and The Hamptons under Aerial Bombardment during the Second World War

by

Paul Barnfield

October 2001
Reprinted 2007

Price £4.50

CONTENTS

Part 1

DEFENCE PREPARATIONS: 1935-1939

Although war was officially declared on September 3rd 1939, preparations had been going ahead for some years in anticipation of hostilities. In response to the possible threat to this country, Britain embarked on re-armament and defence programmes. Experts had earlier calculated that a war would bring horrific casualties from air raids: in the first 24 hours of an attack on the capital, some 1700 persons were expected to be killed, and almost a thousand per day afterwards. The responsibility for the protection of the populace was delegated to the local authorities

In Twickenham, a Committee "to consider the question of local air-raid precautions" was set up in November 1936. By the following year, preparations were in full swing to protect the borough, both civilians and industrial premises, against air attack, to recruit voluntary personnel, to set up groups of rescue and demolition workers, to recruit air-raid precaution (ARP) volunteers and to train them in anti-gas measures. Response, however, was slow to the recruitment drive, and by February 1938 only 165 volunteers had enrolled, and this included one boy of only 11 years! Within months, however, Germany had annexed Austria, and soon had designs on Czechoslovakia, which prompted the Munich Agreement giving the Czech Sudetenland to the Germans. Panic set in as Britain now realised that there was no stopping Hitler's designs on Europe. The Home Office gave immediate instructions to the local authorities to protect the public from probable invasion. Orders were placed immediately for millions of sandbags to protect key buildings against bomb damage, gas masks to protect against the dropping of nerve gas (which was expected following its use during the Civil War in Spain and during the First World War) and large quantities of medical supplies.

Just prior to the emergency, Twickenham had received some 46,800 civilian respirators or gas masks as they were soon to be known; now they were instructed to start fitting them immediately. Within 36 hours, approximately 30,000 persons had been fitted, but some 12,000 were still needed. Orders were placed for large quantities of medical and surgical supplies, and the Teddington Art School in Church Road was taken over as a central store. The first instructions regarding trench digging were also received and local authorities were advised to obtain the necessary timber. Apparently Twickenham had not at this stage agreed to any scheme regarding trenches, so belatedly agreed to order a limited quantity of timber. Two days later digging commenced on three sites - The Green, Murray Park and Elmfield House - all the labour being obtained from labour exchanges. Trench accommodation would soon be available for about 2,700 persons, a little over one-quarter of the total authorised. In Twickenham in the year ending March 1938 only £726 was spent on air-raid precautions; the following year it rose to £16,543; by 1940 it was to soar to almost £200,000.

By January 1939 it was felt that a speed-up of precautions was necessary. Portable steel shelters (later known as Anderson shelters) had been ordered but it was not known exactly when they would be delivered. There was also uncertainty over the supply of sandbags for the protection of shelters - it was estimated that as many as one million of them would be needed for Richmond alone, so Twickenham would need a comparable amount. There was also a definite shortage of air-raid wardens - volunteers had been slow to come forward. The digging of more trenches and the erection of first-aid posts were both still needed. The interest of the public was to be awakened with more anti-gas, first-aid and wardens' courses, and recruiting for the Auxiliary Fire Brigade was to be stepped up. Approval was given for the construction of a trench in York House Gardens and the completion of ones on Twickenham Green and Murray Park. The Twickenham Territorial Unit - the 72nd Middlesex Searchlight Regiment, Royal Artillery - now numbered 648 of the 950 required, and the recruitment of personnel in the National Services as Auxillary Firemen, Air Raid

An A.R.P. warden in full protective kit, Twickenham 1938.
(Courtesy of Richmond Local Studies Collection.)

Wardens, First Aid personnel, drivers, rescue parties, etc., speeded up. It was expected that the issue of gas masks to all residents in Twickenham would be completed by the end of March.

By March, the Borough, now divided into sectors of some 500 individuals for ARP purposes, was advanced enough to give demonstrations of its readiness. For example, in sector "E" of the borough, the wardens had set up their headquarters in a large double-fronted empty shop in Walpole Court, Hampton Road, Twickenham, equipped with suitable publicity and literature and manned by relays of wardens. The walls were lined with lists, regulations and information for the use of wardens. One night the wardens carried out a practice exercise after being given descriptions of imaginary damage supposed to have been done by the bombs of raiding aircraft. Careful records were made of the times taken by the patrols to cover their rounds and report back to the report centre, and then to discuss details of the practice. Great satisfaction was expressed at the results of the exercise. Also at this time it was announced that the Borough was purchasing a trailer gas-chamber in which parties of the public would be able to test the efficiency of their gas-masks in a concentration of tear-gas. It was now estimated that the number of respirators already issued and still to be issued would total some 88,619 plus 4,014 for infants. At the end of March an exercise was held in Richmond Park when volunteer drivers practised driving in the dark without lights and wearing their gas-masks - the purpose of it was to prepare them for the black-out when war came. It was found that, even driving like this, their speed was fairly high.

However, there was not total agreement over all aspects of ARP work. Many of the air-raid wardens demanded a full-time officer and protested that very little progress was being made. But one warden, at least, was full of praise for his fellow wardens. Mr Coney of Bonser Road wrote to the local paper in fulsome praise: :

"I have recently joined the A.R.P. workers, and until I joined up I must confess, like the public, I thought it was a kind of game associated with dinners and convivial gatherings. I have been greatly and agreeably disillusioned, and the way the work is carried on excites my admiration. Every part of the scheme is put forward, threshed out, and executed to the minutest detail. I can best describe it as being done with Germanic thoroughness, harnessed with patriotic equipment. The work of the three sections - the firemen, first-aid, and air-wardens - is daily and nightly progressed, without the general public having much knowledge of their doings. I take off my hat to those local group leaders of ours who are taking off their coats and getting down to their job."

By April, out of 1138 wardens required by the Borough, 803 were trained or being trained, but recruitment for the fire services was much worse - only 608 out of 1360 vacancies had been filled. But the Twickenham Territorial Unit - the Searchlight Regiment - was now up to full strength. By the end of the month the dissatisfaction amongst the wardens felt earlier had intensified even further. At a meeting of the Borough Council protests came from all parts of the Borough on various features of A.R.P. and allegations of "dictatorship" and "totalitarianism" were hurled at the Mayor. Proposals by the Twickenham Communists to provide deep underground shelters for the whole population of the Borough were refused by the Council on grounds of the cost. One complainant to the local paper was very indignant over the Communists' proposal:

> "Who are those Communists who would involve Twickenham district in a modest debt of a million pounds? Very nice of them. Imagine a deep shelter at Twickenham Green, for instance. One would have to be very young and active to dress and get there for a front seat - say from London Road - in seven minutes. How about the elderly and small children? Presumably these are to be pushed out of the way by those young Communists in the scramble for safety. Surely these brave Communists can form a syndicate of their own members to find a bolt hole into which to crawl. We can do without a bomb-proof million pound shelter to save confessed enemies to this Old Country of ours."

By the end of the month it was announced that Twickenham and Richmond would be supplied with Anderson shelters, which would be provided free for people earning under £250 a year and would be erected by the Corporation, who would pay 40 per cent of the cost of putting them up.

By May steady progress was being made in the recruitment of A.R.P workers. One question being raised was the classification of the Borough as a "neutral" area as 90% of the area was residential. The presence of the National Physical Laboratory in Teddington was felt a complication in that it was not easy to see how aircraft travelling at several hundred miles per hour and thousands of feet up, would be able to hit so small a pocket of vulnerable land accurately, and the proposals to dig public trenches in Bushy Park, a few seconds flying time away from the vulnerable spot, was felt ill-advised at the least. Indeed this was to be tragically realised in November 1940 when this very nightmare occurred. Concern was still being expressed over the lack of wardens and other A.R.P. workers in some parts of the Borough - complaints were made of "unpatriotic grousers who won't work" and of "streets of idlers". By the end of the month residents were invited to apply for the issue of the Anderson shelters. "But don't ask when you will get your shelter. Nobody knows", they were told.

By July tenders were being invited for the erection of wardens' posts. Some 78 were needed for the Borough, at a cost not exceeding £50 each.

In the middle of August a full-scale rehearsal of a complete black-out of Richmond, Twickenham and neighbouring districts was carried out. Although there was some confusion among A.R.P. workers, it was judged an almost

A.R.P. demonstrations outside York House, Twickenham 1938. (Courtesy Richmond Local Studies Collection.)

complete success, although the black-out was not so thorough as desired. Housewives were also being informed of the government's plans to introduce rationing: meat, bacon and ham, sugar, butter, margarine and cooking fats would be brought immediately into a rationing scheme and individuals would have to register at a retail shop for each rationed food. Wardens' posts were in the course of erection and trench-digging had been accelerated, especially on Twickenham Green.

By the end of the month war seemed imminent and full-scale contingency plans were put into operation. The Chertsey Road was one of nine major roads leading out of London which was made one-way for several days so that there would be no obstacle to evacuation and other traffic leaving London. Thousands of children passed through Richmond station on their evacuation from London; some 25,000 of them left for Reading. The Lord Privy Seal gave urgent advice if an air attack occurred :

"Anyone who has an Anderson shelter properly earthed over is virtually secure from anything except a direct hit, or its equivalent. Therefore, any one who has a shelter not yet erected should see to its erection at once. Those who have no garden shelters can obtain a considerable degree of protection by digging a trench in the garden with 18in. of overhead earth cover. The best place inside the house is the basement or, if there is no basement, the ground floor. Choose a passage or a room with a small window for the place of refuge, especially if it looks out on a narrow passage. Anyone who is out of doors should follow any signs leading to public basements or trenches. Do not in any event remain standing or running about in the street."

The Richmond and Twickenham Times reported on the Borough's response just a few days after the declaration of war on 3rd September:

"With a quiet, dignified loyalty Twickenham responded to the call which came on Sunday morning, when the Prime Minister told a troubled world that at last this country had been compelled to declare war on Germany. The suspense of the last few weeks gave place to a feeling almost of relief. That war was imminent was seen in the speed-up made all last week in the digging of trenches and the other services undertaken under the direction of York House. Wednesday's early siren did not take Twickenham unawares, and the months of devoted work that have been put into the Borough's A.R.P. scheme by paid and voluntary workers now gains its own reward in the potential protection of 100,000 people. It will be appreciated at once with the tremendous feats of organisation that modern war entails, all has not yet been done. But throughout this week there has been working, 24 hours a day, a service run by men and women whose varied tasks will provide protection for everybody, if and when bombers come, on a scale never dreamed of in wars of the past."

The public were assured that over sixty places of shelter would soon be available throughout the Borough in the event of an air-raid. One of the largest shelters in the Borough - with accommodation for 700 - was rapidly approaching completion in Clifden Road. At the Green there would soon be a shelter for 620, with others for 300 in Kneller Gardens and for 250 at Moor Mead. Almost ready for completion were shelters under the railway arches in Heath Road (400) and in Popes Grove (200). Shelters fully completed were at Marble Hill (355), York House (180), Murray Park (200) and Home Park (160). Trenches were also well in hand at various sites across the Borough and a number of basement premises had been or were being converted into public shelters.

Although Richmond started receiving its Anderson steel shelters in mid-July, Twickenham did not receive its first consignment of 730 until the end of October - 530 for Twickenham and 200 for Teddington. Residents of the Hamptons would have to wait for theirs, as another nine thousand were still needed to satisfy the Borough's needs. Ration books, some 92,000 altogether, were almost ready for distribution to every household in the Borough.

By the end of December, some 2,245 Anderson shelters had been delivered, about one-third of the needs of the Borough. There was now accommodation for nearly 7,500 people in trenches, basements and public shelters. Total accommodation planned would be 12,058 or some 12% of the peacetime population of the Borough.

So ended 1939 with frantic efforts to protect the residents and businesses of the Borough from aerial bombardment but, as yet, no sign of the long expected bombing.

§

Part 2

UNDER ATTACK : AUGUST 1940 - MAY 1941

i : Waiting for attack and the first bomb on the Borough

To those living in England, the first eight months of the War was an uneasy period of waiting. People experienced all the sensations of war - rationing, blackouts and evacuation - without the fighting, a period nicknamed the Phoney War.

In Twickenham good progress was being made in the provision of air-raid protection. The delivery of Anderson shelters continued gradually: by May 1940 some 6,305 had been delivered, with only 99 more needed. As far as communal shelters were concerned, by September 1940 when Twickenham was finally directly affected by the War, some 57 were open to the public accommodating some 2,888 people, while another 69 holding 2,822 were in course of erection. There was now public accommodation for some 11,799 persons - 8,394 in trench and surface shelters, 1,728 in basements, 672 in railway arches, 444 in bridge arches and 565 in temporary trenches. At the beginning of 1940 rescue parties had been fixed at ten light and two heavy parties, a total personnel of 128. Eight of the parties were stationed at London Road, Twickenham and three at Oldfield Road, Hampton. The decontamination centre, to clean protective clothing affected by gas attacks, was to be erected at the Twickenham refuse works. By the middle of June total personnel of the supplementary fire parties was 1,007 of whom 309 were fully trained, and equipped with 47 pumps. In the early summer incendiary bomb demonstrations were held on Twickenham Embankment, and an order was placed for the supply of 500 stirrup pumps for re-sale to the public at one guinea each.

At the end of March a big re-organisation of the A.R.P. in Twickenham took place, which largely meant a reduction in staffing levels, due to the authorities' concern at the huge expense of keeping a large force of paid and volunteer staff on constant stand-by for months on end.

Despite the general unity amongst everyone in the war effort, there was not always complete harmony in the ranks. *The Evening News,* for example, reported the story of twelve wardens who resigned from their post at Whitton in November 1939. They complained that they were ordered about *"in a manner used to naughty children and halfwits"*; and *"We were inundated with orders and counter-orders in the same breath. Squads which had worked together were repeatedly broken up, first-aid equipment was frequently locked away or lost, and until recently there was a general lack of organisation and we had no beds. We could also tell of stinking blankets and many small oppressions of being awakened from sleep to hear some trivial order".*

However, the time of waiting for attack - the Phoney War - was not to last indefinitely. In June 1940, following his conquest of France, Hitler turned his attention to England and the Luftwaffe attempted to destroy the RAF to obtain air superiority over the Channel, so that England could be invaded by sea. At first the battles took place over South East England and the Channel, but victory was coming too slowly for Hitler. He had always been reluctant to have London bombed - he wanted to have it intact when he marched in triumph through the city after England's surrender - but an incident on August 24 was to change his mind with devastating consequences for London. That night six German bombers were ordered to bomb the oil refineries at Thames Haven on the outskirts of London. Some of their bombs did find their mark, but, because it was a cloudy night, they could not see their targets and instead they dropped most of their bombloads over the centre of London. Churchill immediately ordered reprisals against Berlin and one hundred British bombers were despatched to bomb the German capital. It was not a great success and Berlin was not badly hit, but Hitler immediately ordered Goering to retaliate on British cities, to bomb them into submission. So night after night for some nine months London was attacked with the full force of the Luftwaffe and there seemed very little to stop the German bombers. The RAF were powerless to stop the night-raids and the anti-aircraft guns and barrage balloons had little effect. In London alone, during this period that became known as the Blitz, some 20,000 people were to lose their lives while hundreds of thousands of homes were destroyed and damage to property was astronomical.

The first bomb to fall on the Borough fell on August 24th 1940, probably one of the bombs intended for the oil refineries at Thames Haven. At twelve minutes to midnight a high explosive bomb landed on 153 Tudor Avenue, Hampton, the home of Frederick William Reynolds and his wife. A photograph in *The Richmond & Twickenham Times* showed this very first incident and the devastation it caused - the house reduced to rubble. Mr Reynolds was also the very first casualty through bombing - he was rushed to Mogden Hospital where he remained until he was discharged some seven weeks later. The occupants seemed to have had miraculous escapes: they had just got out of the back door on their way to their Anderson shelter when the bomb fell. Mr Reynolds was flung through a privet hedge into the next garden while Mrs Reynolds was buried under the bath, the rest of the contents of the bathroom, the gas stove and an electric copper from the kitchen and the back door. Yet both escaped with nothing more serious than shock, lacerations and bruises.

Where the first bomb fell in the Borough, on August 24th 1940: the home of Mr and Mrs Frederick Reynolds in Tudor Road, Hampton. (Courtesy Richmond Local Studies Collection)

ii : September 1940

Almost two weeks later, on September 6 and just one day before the main Luftwaffe attack on London, incendiary bombs were dropped on ten places in Teddington and Twickenham. From then on, on most nights, the Borough was to suffer aerial bombardment on varying scales, sometimes lightly, sometimes on a horrific scale. The attacks did not diminish until December, but still continued intermittently until the end of May 1941.

In September 1940 there were some 274 incidents, the official term given to the occasion or event of a bomb being dropped. During the month some 57 high-explosive bombs were dropped, as well as 7 oil-bombs and 84 groups of incendiaries.

The first fatality of the War occurred on the night of 13 September when Joan Olive, aged 18, was killed at her home at 89 Godstone Road, St Margarets. She was killed instantly by a missile that penetrated their ground floor flat while she was still holding her pet cat. But an elderly couple, living in the same house, slept through the disturbance, even when the wardens broke open their door.

On the night of September 16 Twickenham experienced a very bad night of aerial bombardment. At 10.30 pm a 250 kg delayed-action high-explosive bomb dropped on Radnor House in Cross Deep. It penetrated to the cellar, exploded two hours later and reduced the mansion to a heap of rubble. Donald Simpson, then living nearby in Holmes Road, heard the bomb come down and then explode a few hours later. "It was a curious effect - Radnor House wasn't scattered all over the place. It was as though it blew up and fell in - the rubble was all contained on the site of the house".

Wardens who were helping to evacuate neighbours fortunately heard the rumble of explosion in time and ordered everyone to lie down, so that there were no casualties. The convent school nearby was damaged and had to be closed for the time being. Another bomb dropped the same evening demolished all the houses between Radnor House and Ryan House - River View Cottage, Cross Deep Hall, Beechcroft and River Deep. Radnor House was probably built in the late seventeenth century but extensively remodelled in an Italianate style in the mid-nineteenth century. It was acquired by the Twickenham Urban District Council in 1902 but fell into disrepair. Proposals were made to renovate it but the Council was loathe to spend funds, so that when news of the demise of Radnor House reached the Council chamber at their meeting, it was recorded that there was a loud cheer as they were now not liable for any further expenses. Today the grounds of Radnor House, together with those of the adjoining bomb-damaged houses, are open to the public as Radnor Gardens.

Two days later four people were killed in Broom Road, Teddington, when a high-explosive bomb fell on numbers 122 and 124. It was probably this incident that Verena Simmons (living in Kingston Road) was referring to in one of her letters to her sisters in Westmorland on September 21. *"Unfortunately there were casualties 2 nights ago (in) Broom Rd, which runs parallel with Kingston rd. only nearer the river. We think that Jerry imagines the refuse destructor is a water works, for he has peppered that district 3 times. It is surrounded by fields and only the one got a house and smashed every window."*

The night of September 25/26 was especially bad - there were some 75 incidents, but luckily no fatalities. But three nights later a high-explosive bomb dropped behind Twickenham Green killing two men passing the Baptist Church.

The last day of the month was also a bad night for the Borough. Another high-explosive bomb fell on 5 and 7 Bloxham Crescent in Hampton killing a widow and her two children and a woman next door.

For many in the Borough circumstances brought about new routines, especially at night-time when most of the air-raids occurred. For those with Anderson shelters in their gardens, sleeping comfortably in them at night could be a problem and took getting used to. But Mrs Simmons of Teddington wrote how *"remarkably easy one becomes used to things. As soon as supper - of necessity at seven, is over - there is a rush to clear ... and have all to hand for the alarm, which comes pretty regularly at 8.15. Then out we come (to our dug-out in the garden). Equipped with sewing, wireless set, writing or books, and plus hot bottles ... We have the wireless and listen if we want, but if the guns are pretty active I prefer to hear rather than stretch one's ears through another sound, as it is necessary to listen in case incendiaries come. Then we sew or play chess or read until about 11, and then put up Leonard's campbed and lay out my rolled mattress and go to sleep in the hole, which is dry and warm and fairly comfortable apart from not being able to stand upright in it. My evening garments are now, knickers, pyjamas and a thick dark green siren suit, which I change into at six, and Leonard* (her husband) *has pyjamas, trousers and a thick sweater. I believe the all clear generally goes about six, but sleep through it, and emerge about 8 o'clock. It is a marvellous saving in laundry of sheets, and I am forgetting how to make proper beds, as ours consist of rugs and pillows covered in gingham for the shelter, and are all quickly folded up and stowed on the bench."* For others without Anderson shelters, it might mean sleeping under the stairs, under a Morrison shelter (a table of steel with sides of wire mesh) or even under a billiard table, as Donald Simpson recalls.

iii : October 1940

October saw a slight decrease in the number of incidents, but a significant change in the proportions of bombs dropped - fewer incendiaries but more high-explosive bombs (69). Consequently the number of fatalities was to increase from twelve in September to sixteen in October.

On the night of October 7 a young man from Constance Road staying at 34 Tranmere Road, Whitton, was killed by an exploding shell. Then three nights later a couple living in Fulwell Road, Teddington, were killed by a high-explosive bomb exploding in Clonmel Road, and on the same night a lady staying at 71 Whitton Dene was killed by another bomb landing on numbers 71 and 73. The next night a high-explosive bomb landed in Warfield Road, Hampton, at the junction of Station Road, demolishing most of the houses on the west side of Warfield Road and most of the houses in Station Road between the Worlds End and the Railway Inn. Four people died that night, three in Warfield Road and one in Station Road. And on the same night another high-explosive bomb fell on numbers 71 to 93 Uxbridge Road, seriously damaging six house but causing only minor casualties.

Three nights later another bomb fell on "Show Boat" in the Hampton Court Road, killing a woman at "Tamesis" in the same road. On the 19th of the month the Blandford Road shelter at Teddington was hit and one, possibly two, people were killed. And on the same night another bomb hit the Rosslyn Road area of East Twickenham, killing a woman at 22 St Margarets Road.

Bombs continued to fall night after night, but miraculously most proved to be non-fatal, although many people had to be sent to hospital through injuries sustained.

In September eighteen persons needed to be kept in hospital, in October thirty-seven and this was set to rise to some eighty-three in November.

Mrs Simmons of Teddington continued to relate her day-to-day life to her sisters in Westmorland :

"The night before a shell - not a bomb, came through the house nearly opposite and exploded in the cellar, and slightly injured the old things living there - the very thin man and the very fat woman. We heard the bang but it was not half as loud as bombs that have fallen much further off, and we knew nothing about it until next day, and the night before that there were about 50 incendiaries on streets about ½ mile away - all put out in five minutes, but the smell was like 5th November. They tell us we must expect more damage here as the barrage has been much strengthened round about, and that often means dropping bombs to get away from it. However if it saves poor London a little, we can take it quite well.

"Yesterday was a bad day altogether, as we had gun and air battery 3 times during the day, and usually the alarms are nothing more in day time. It is horribly annoying, as now I don't feel I can go out shopping as I used to if there happened to be an alarm."

The end of October saw one more fatal incident. On the 25th one or two high-explosive bombs fell in Nelson Road, Whitton, near the corner of Constance Road. Four people living in 243 and 245 Nelson Road were killed and at least eight houses, as well as the temporary Roman Catholic church of St Edmonds, were so seriously damaged that they had to be rebuilt. The church, only five years old, was burned to the ground, only the brick walls, the charred roof beams and blackened steel girders remaining. The flames spread so quickly that all the fire brigade could do was concentrate on saving the school which lay just behind the church.

Excitement was caused by the River Thames at Teddington at the end of the month when a high-explosive bomb landed on part of the apron of the Weir. The bomb apparently penetrated the apron before exploding. The breach in the weir caused a reduction of depth of water in the reach by about six feet, making navigation for barges impossible except at high tides. It was estimated that repair works would take about seven weeks before full navigation in the reach would be restored. Vera Simmons wrote of this :

"The latest excitement here is to go and see the river. A bomb - small one - breached the top of the island at one side of the weir, with a result that the reach above shrunk at once and all boatmen have become beachcombers for what they have lost in the mud in past years. The explosion threw up an immense amount of stones all over the place and many windows in the weir direction have gone of course. Trowlock Island people were marooned until planks could be found to cross the backwater."

iv : November 1940

The first five days of November were ominously quiet - no bombs at all being dropped - but this was not to last and the last few nights of the month were to see the worst bombing of the War. During the whole of November there were some 374 incidents, but of these 224 were to occur on the one night of November 29/30. Of the 74 or more fatalities, at least 61 were to die on that one fateful night.

On the night of November 7 Hampton was badly hit by eight high-explosive bombs. One of them landed in Dean Road killing one person and another landed on the "White House" killing a husband and wife and their 14 year old son inside and two others in Oak Avenue.

The next night it was Whitton's turn to be hit - eight high-explosive bombs were dropped on it, one of which killed a 35 year old man at 88 Hounslow Road. The following night it was both Hampton and Teddington's turns to suffer - eleven high explosives were dropped on the towns. One dropped in Falcon Road, Hampton, killing a couple at their home at number 27.

For a few nights raids on the area were light - in fact the main incident was when a British Wellington bomber crashed onto 63 Park Road, Hampton Hill, the home of Lady Stanton. The crew had luckily baled out previously when the plane had become uncontrollable due to icing, and no-one in the house was hurt although it was completely gutted. The ammunition from the Wellington's guns kept exploding in the heat of the fire caused by the crash and caused alarm in the neighbourhood as it sounded as if enemy aircraft were machine-gunning the fire.

Then on the following night German aircraft dropped two landmines on Hampton Hill. One dropped in Alpha Road, exploded and killed four people outright. Another person, seriously injured, died in hospital soon after. There were quite a few serious injuries as some were trapped in the debris. The damage caused in the road was very severe and numbers 8 to 20 were so seriously damaged that they had to be demolished. They were never rebuilt and there is a large gap in the road where the houses used to stand. An hour later the other landmine was discovered, unexploded, behind 17 High Street, Hampton Hill. Both Marjorie Price and Henry Pease remember seeing this landmine, suspended in a tree and dangling by its cords. A wide area around it was cordoned off and rapidly evacuated and a specialist bomb-disposal unit called in which successfully defused it. Mrs Simmons also witnessed this incident and wrote of it to her sisters :

"A week ago there was a land mine dropped on the way to Hampton Hill, and they are really dreadful things - about 100 houses are quite unfit for habitation, and hundreds more had all their windows blown away. As it is a thickly populated district, there's about ½ a mile radius smashed in some way, but fortunately few casualties. There was a second mine, quite near to the Milligans and many other friends of mine - whose houses would have all been ruined, but these things come down in parachutes and it was hung up in a tree and did not explode most luckily."

The night of November 18 saw nine high-explosive bombs dropped over Twickenham, but this time without any serious casualties. Then there was eight days' respite from bombing before the area suffered from the worst and most devastating bombardment from the air during the whole War on the night of November 29/30. It was to be a night that many residents of the Borough remember vividly to this day. That night alone, over 130 high-explosive bombs were dropped, as well as some three to five thousand incendiaries and two oil-bombs. The Imperial War Graves Commission has listed 61 names of people killed in the former Borough on that night, but hospital records indicate that this figure could be as high as 68. Approximately 150 dwelling houses were completely destroyed, 350 more were severely damaged and at least 6,000 slightly damaged that night.

The raid started at about 7 pm when a large number of incendiaries were dropped followed by all sizes of high explosives. The whole Borough was affected, but Teddington most severely, followed by Twickenham in intensity. In Teddington, Church Road was probably the worst hit and the most badly damaged. At the Willoughby Arms public house, on the corner of Argyle Road, eight people were killed including the licensee Frank Tomlin and his two children. It took at least four days to find all the bodies and get them all out of the debris. In Church Road, between Walpole Road and Somerset Road, most of the houses were badly damaged and another ten people killed. At no.55 a

The Willoughby Hotel, Teddington, where 8 people died on the night of November 29/30th 1940. (Courtesy Ken Howe)

married couple and their 18 year old son were killed, and next door, at no.57, so were a married couple and their 6 year old son. On the other side of Walpole Road the Baptist Church was hit and, because the fire-fighting services were unable to cope with such a conflagration, people could only watch helplessly while the Church burnt itself out. The minister of the church, the Rev. Sutton, had only started his ministry there four weeks previously, but he soon set about rallying the membership around him to repair the damage. In fact, the very next day after the church was left with only the walls standing, one of the youngest members of the congregation knocked at the door of the minister's house and said, "Please, here's a shilling for the new church". Services were held in the Sunday School buildings which escaped fairly lightly, until a new church building was opened in 1956.

In Railway Road which runs parallel to Church Road, numbers 31 to 35 were hit and five people here died - a married couple and their 14 year old son at no.32 and a married couple next door at no.33. These houses have never been rebuilt. Not far away in Shacklegate Lane a large stretch of terraced houses, nos. 54 to 76, were so badly damaged that they were demolished and, likewise, they have never been rebuilt. On their site today there are just garages. Thirteen people died in this one stretch, including a mother and her three very young children at no. 62 and a mother and her two children aged 4 and 6 at no. 66.

One of the other great tragedies that night was when nine 500 kg high explosive bombs rained down at 9 pm around the National Physical Laboratory buildings. Fortunately only slight damage was done to the NPL but two of the bombs exploded near the public shelter in the grounds and eight people were killed as a result of the blasts. One of the bombs exploded 18 feet from the entrance to the underground trench shelter and made a crater 42 feet across. This shelter, which was 6ft 8in high and 4ft 8in wide internally was lined with concrete walls 4½ in thick and the roof was 6in thick. Nine-inch thick brick walls shielding the entrance were completely demolished. The other bomb exploded near the other end of the shelter and made a crater 45 ft across. The roof of the trench and about 34 ft of the length of the wall caved in. Six people were killed instantly and three seriously injured, of whom two died subsequently. Those who died all lived in Walpole Crescent - Annie Rumble and her two sons from no.15 and the other three from no.10.

Considerable damage was caused to local power supplies and large parts of the area were without supply for days. In Latimer road only minor damage was caused to Stanley Electrical Works but incendiaries dropped on the Baltic Timber Yard in Stanley Road set the yard alight and the resultant blaze could be seen for miles. The final fatality that night in Teddington and the Fulwell area was when a lady was killed at her home at no.14 Links View Road by a high explosive bomb.

In Twickenham, Gravel Road was badly hit when a high explosive bomb landed on nos. 1-3; three people were killed in these houses. In the Meadway one person was killed at no.52 and two more around the corner in Staines Road. Another high-explosive landed at the junction of Egerton Road and Heathfield North, killing a man at no. 25 Egerton Road. In Albert Road another high-explosive killed five people living in nos. 28, 30, 32 and 36, and in Wellesley Crescent yet another high-explosive killed a further three, including a couple at no.10. At St Margarets in Kenley Road a couple at no.79 were killed by a high-explosive, as was also a man at his house at 21 Tranmere Road in Whitton. Another bomb dropped on the railway line near the Chertsey Road bridge between Twickenham and Whitton stations damaging the track so much that services had to be suspended. Small fires were caused in the Maternity Ward of St John's Hospital, set alight by incendiaries, and patients had to be evacuated to Mogden Hospital. At the York House Municipal Offices, the council chambers were damaged by fire, and incendiaries dropped in the Copthall Gardens area slightly damaged the Poppe Rubber Factory in Sherland Road. Incendiaries were also dropped on St Mary's College in Waldegrave Road, but seem to have been quickly extinguished.

The morning after the raid, November 30, Teddington and Twickenham looked a scene of devastation. Almost every road was affected in one way or another. Waldegrave Road, Twickenham, between Cross Deep and Waldegrave Park, was blocked by a large crater. Many other roads were pitted with craters and many more closed for fear of setting off unexploded bombs.

Mrs Lilian Dring well remembers that night :

"There will be many who remember the terrible night of November 29, 1940, when most of Teddington became a raging inferno. Duty rotas were abandoned and every available warden was on duty most of the night. This was the night when the Baltic timber yard, Stanley Road (and now council flats near the corner of Walpole Road) and the Baptist Church (Church Road) went up in mountains of flame which almost met over our heads as we patrolled in Walpole Road. And there was no water !

"This was the night when families from Walpole Crescent (just under the blazing church) were evacuated to a "safe" shelter in the N.P.L. grounds - which later had a direct hit. Among the victims were the wife and two young sons of one of our colleagues, Mr Rumble, the plumber - on duty with us all night, wondering, between "incidents", where his family had been evacuated. It was morning before he found out.

"This was the night when high explosive bombs rained down on the area

High Street, Whitton,
after being hit by a
doodle bug, June 19th 1944.
(Courtesy Vic Rosewarne)

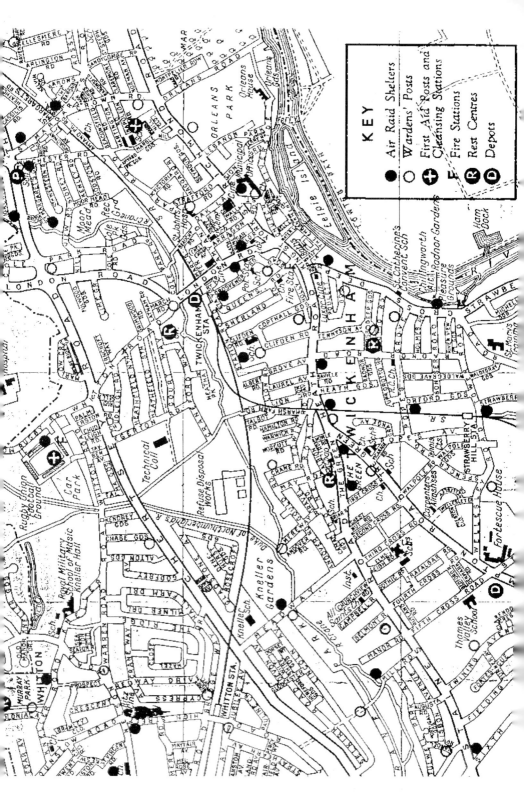

KEY

●	Air Raid Shelters
○	Wardens' Posts
✚	First Aid Posts and Cleansing Stations
F	Fire Stations
R	Rest Centres
D	Depots

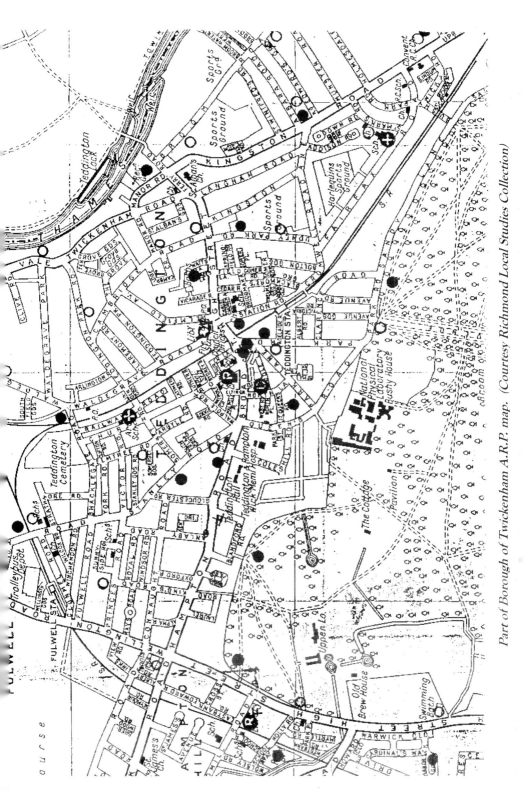

Part of Borough of Twickenham A.R.P. map. (Courtesy Richmond Local Studies Collection)

Argyle Road, Teddington, after the doodle bug attack in July 1944 (Courtesy Paddy Ching)

including over 100 delayed action bombs in and around Bushy Park which was afterwards closed for a week while these were disposed of. Another delayed action bomb fell 'somewhere in Hampton Road'. I remember the sensation (while my husband and I were taking a very brief respite in our coal cellar-cum-shelter at no.34) of the brick walls seeming to expand and contract again with the impact, and although our corner of Hampton Road / Gloucester Road was 'roped off' for several days, the bomb was never found. I wonder if it is still there?

"This was the night when The Willoughby in Church Road received a direct hit killing a number of people who had assembled at a meeting there, and half of Argyle Road was demolished. Then local doctors performed hazardous operations to release those still alive but trapped in the tottering buildings.

"I well remember the 'Christmas card' effect of the dust-covered roofs and roads - so white and thick it looked like snow - and how, when we fell flat because of a 'passing bomb', we were white with dust when rising. Someone even said: 'It's snowing', but it was only the dust, dust, dust of shattered buildings."

Verena Simmons described the happenings of that night to her sisters:

"I am afraid I spoke too soon about the planes passing over last night - by 7.30 it was getting very unpleasant. Sylvie and I spent a lot of time under the dining room table, as bombs were dropping two or three every ten minutes or so, and being indoors it did not seem wise to try to go out. At last there was one very near which burst open the doors and windows and we heard things dropping in the house - pieces of plaster discharged we thought. I didn't like to investigate upstairs as I could feel windows were open to the air and thought a torch might show, so we got our coats and ran for the shelter... There was a big fire just the other side of the railway bridge and everything as bright as day with fire and flares; and a heavy ground frost. The all clear went about 2.0 ... I don't think there is a pane of glass left in High Street, the Baptist Church where the Guild meets is down, several houses round about, and several craters in the roads, and unfortunately they evacuated a whole slum dwelling to the shelter at the lab, and a minute after the shelter got a direct hit. The Lab is not injured beyond broken windows and sweeping glass where ever you go. We have not heard about other damage or casualties yet, but there must be a lot over Teddington, Twickenham and Richmond, which seemed to be the selected target."

The Borough came under some criticism because of a breakdown in communications that night. During the raid it was estimated that some 2000 messages passed through the Twickenham Report Centre. But after the preliminary report of bombing in the Borough, no further damage reports whatsoever were relayed to Subgroup headquarters. Consequently they did not realise the seriousness of the situation until midnight when it was too late to send stand-by rescue parties. Nonetheless it was found that the services worked very well at the incidents; rescue work and the recovery of bodies proceeded well for three or four days after the raid. It was regretted that in spite of mutual assistance exercises, Twickenham did not make application soon enough or for sufficient help. But fortunately no lives were lost through this and the only result was the overworking of the Twickenham rescue parties. Twickenham was duly reprimanded and promised to set its house in order. Twickenham was praised, however, for its organisation for Feeding and Rest Centres. It was noted that all homeless people were billeted within 36 hours, and the removal of furniture dealt with very quickly, aided by furniture vans from as far afield as Bushey in Hertfordshire.

It was noted in the same report that, although bombing appeared to be generally indiscriminate, direct hits by both incendiaries and high explosive bombs were scored on the Royal Naval College at St Margarets, although the building was not of naval importance but merely a school for the daughters of naval officers. It seems much more likely that the targets that night were the N.P.L. (where Barnes Wallis was working on the design of the Bouncing Bomb, used so successfully by the Dambusters in May 1943) and possibly Tough Brothers' boatyard in Teddington. All through the War this firm produced various types of light warships and also, most surprisingly, midget submarines for the Pacific campaign. It has been suggested that this was why the area around Tough's was attacked so heavily. Richmond, too, was very badly bombed that night and the reason that this town was probably singled out for attention by the bombers was that within the walls of Richmond Park worked some of Britain's leading scientists, working out problems that ranged from the beginning of radar - radio location - to land-mine detection and that the Germans had an inkling of the important research being carried out here.

v : December 1940 - May 1941

After the terrible bombardment that the Borough - especially Teddington - had suffered on the night of November 29/30, the area seems to have been given time to recover and recuperate, and although it was to suffer sporadic bombing over the next seven months, certainly the worst was over for the Borough. The same could not be said, of course, for London as a whole.

Just after Christmas, on the night of Sunday December 29, saw what became known as the "Second Great Fire of London", when some 127 tons of high explosives and more than 10,000 incendiaries were dropped around the St Paul's area of the City. The last major raid on London on May 10 produced the largest number of casualties for any night of the Blitz - 1436 dead and 1792 seriously injured. That night alone some 700 tons of high-explosive and 100,000 incendiaries were dropped, mainly around the docks and the East End, and damage was very severe, including more than 5,000 houses destroyed.

Apart from perhaps one high-explosive bomb dropped on the Hampton Court Road on December 11, no bombing seems to have occurred over the Borough during the last month of 1940, although there was much work to be done clearing and defusing the unexploded bombs dropped during the November raids. Sometimes these UXBs were not discovered for months, even years. For example there were several found in Home Park that were not cleared until February 1941 and one unexploded 259 kg bomb at the rear of a house in Waldegrave Road, Teddington, was discovered by a gardener cutting down bushes months after it had fallen. Defusing the unexploded bombs was a very hazardous and dangerous operation: six men and their officer lost their lives on December 10 whilst removing UXB's in Chestnut Avenue in Bushy Park.

In January of the New Year, 1941, the raiders returned on the 9th dropping incendiaries over a wide area of south Teddington. More were dropped in the afternoon of the 31st around the St Stephen's Church area of East Twickenham. An incendiary actually hurtled through the roof of the church and exploded in a pew. The verger, Mr Bray, was the hero of the day when he speedily extinguished it and his actions were put into verse by one of his grateful congregation :

> "Saint Stephen's Church shall be my prey !
> Within God's House my flames I'll play !
> Thus Satan spake; but Verger Bray
> With Christian zeal, quenched Hell that day."

On the 8th March two high-explosive bombs were dropped, both landing in Marble Hill Park and fortunately causing no damage or casualties. But two days later two more fell in Collingwood Close, Whitton. Both landed on concrete roads about 50 yards apart and exploded, causing very severe damage to 130 houses and lesser damage to many more. The fact that they appear to have exploded together accounted for the large amount of damage by blast. It completely destroyed a brick and concrete shelter which fortunately was unoccupied at the time. Miraculously there were no fatalities, but ten people were severely injured and another eight slightly.

The next day two 500 kg bombs fell in Whitton, one in Constance Road and the other in Mayfair Avenue. Fortunately both landed in back gardens and both failed to explode, so no damage was caused.

The next month, April, saw another raid on the 17th, when two high explosives were dropped, again harmlessly, one in Home Park in plantations and the other in the River Thames nearby. Verena Simmons wrote to her sisters of that night :

"It is a bad night. I fear poor London is having a dreadful time. There must be huge fires in the dock district, and earlier there were flares and incendiaries somewhere southeast of Kingston. The roar of planes has never stopped since nine last night, and guns have been busy nearly all the time, and for the last hour often heavy concussions which make no noise but shake everything. I am afraid it means very heavy stuff is being dropped on London. I slept in rugs from 11.30 to 1.30 and then got up and made tea and went to visit the other watchers to tell them they could go off duty - feeling weighed down by a ridiculous tin hat.

"Now 5.0 a.m. and the all clear and I can go to sleep - but poor London. There are huge banks of red smoke all over the east in an otherwise clear sky. The worst fires we have had yet I should say and a very long heavy raid."

It was indeed a bad night for London - the heaviest air attack on London to date - when nearly 900 tons of high explosives and more than 100,000 incendiaries were dropped on the capital. Nearly 1200 people lost their lives that night.

Earlier that year Mrs Simmons wrote of the damage done to her home town:

"Teddington is a disgrace and looks more so in this sunshine. More and more empty shops and if they have not been shocked by bombs they are just left in a mess. Those that are open have good shutters, but not so the empties into which any unsuitable person could get easily - and filthy. Poor Eric had his store bombed and burnt out last Saturday and the nightwatchman killed. He is busy salvaging and giving the stuff away to slum people nearabout now. He expects to be called up in a month or so."

On the last major raid on the capital and the suburbs on May 10/11 which produced fatalities of 1,436 dead, the Borough came off very lightly.

Incendiaries were dropped around the Powder Mill Lane area of Whitton and a high-explosive bomb was dropped in Hanworth Road, but there seem to have been no casualties. This was the last major attack on the Borough in this phase of the War, although an "own goal" was scored on the 19th August when a Spitfire crash-landed in Ormond Crescent, Hampton. The job still remained, however of clearing up all the debris from the previous months' raids and dealing with all the unexploded bombs, shells and missiles lying around.

§

The Beaufort Works on the edge of Marble Hill after bombing on November 29/30th 1940. (Courtesy Richmond Local Studies Collection)

Part 3

RESPITE FROM ATTACK :
JUNE 1941 - DECEMBER 1943

From June 1941 attacks on England continued, but on a very much reduced scale. The German Luftwaffe was concentrating its efforts on the attack on Russia and its squadrons were much reduced in numbers because rates of production could not keep up with losses. During the years 1942 and 1943 there were less than thirty raids on London, and of these only one reached Twickenham. On the night of the April 20th 1943 a lone two-engined plane flying at some 30,000 feet came in from the east before passing towards Slough. It was a perfect night for bombing - a full moon, no cloud and no wind. The German aircraft dropped a 500 kg high explosive bomb over Twickenham which luckily missed any houses and fell on a footpath just east of Cambridge Park. Some 30 feet of brick walling was demolished, a 3" water main was fractured and some thirty houses suffered glass damage.

§

Radnor House, Twickenham, after being bombed in September 1940. (Courtesy Richmond Local Studies Collection)

Part 4

THE LITTLE BLITZ : JANUARY - MARCH 1944

The beginning of 1944 saw the period known as the Little Blitz as the Luftwaffe had now managed to assemble a force of over 500 aircraft in Northern France. There were several light raids in January but also a much larger one on the 21st when some 447 aircraft attacked Southern England. But because many of the new German crew were relatively inexperienced, the attack failed mainly due to bad navigation. Only one bomb fell over the Borough this month, but this fortunately exploded in mid-air over Thames Ditton Island and caused no damage, although fragments were scattered over a wide area.

For several months the attacks continued using a variety of bombs. Miraculously most of those that fell over the Borough landed on open land, so physical damage to property was relatively minor and only two persons lost their lives.

At the beginning of February two high explosive bombs fell in Home Park, the only damage caused being broken glass to houses in the Portsmouth Road in Kingston. The end of the month saw several days of heavy bombing. It started on the 20th with two bombs dropped close together, one in the centre of the Chertsey Road just north of the railway bridge and the other on the railway embankment just west of the bridge. Then early in the morning of the 23rd four bombs fell in the Cemetery and allotments near the junction of Hanworth Road and Powder Mill Lane, and one fell south of the Staines Road in Fulwell Park. Of these five, three failed to explode. In the evening of the same day a mine was dropped in a garden on the east side of Clarence Road in Teddington. There was also a large number of incendiary bombs dropped over the centre of Hampton Wick. Bombs fell in Station Road, Vicarage Road, Park Road, Upper Teddington Road and High Street. Fires were started but seem to have been quickly extinguished, but a visitor from West Byfleet was killed outside the railway station. At the same time a further large number of incendiaries were dropped over Ripley Road, Priory Road and Oldfield Road in Hampton. Again no serious fires resulted.

On the 25th of that month, some 45 bombs were dropped over the Borough. It was a fine, clear, starry night, with only a slight wind, but no moon. The affected area stretched from the Chertsey Road in the north, to Home Park in the south, Oldfield Road in the west and to Broom Road, Teddington, to the east. A number of the bombs fell close to the National Physical Laboratory, one just to the north-east in Queen's Road and five others in Chestnut Avenue, Bushy Park, near to the main gate in Park Road and very close to the American military camp. Observers stated that the enemy aircraft approached from the south and then seemed to circle round Twickenham before dropping their flares. By the light of these the enemy dropped their deadly cargo before heading southwards back home. This time it does seem that the enemy had Teddington as its prime target - the NPL and American base in Bushy Park. A cocktail of bombs was dropped - 50 kg phosphate, high explosive bombs of 50kg, 250kg, 500kg and 1,000kg, as well as incendiaries. Three bombs fell in Fulwell Golf Course and 28 over Hampton and Hampton Hill, 15 of which fell on nurseries. The damage caused in all these cases was only slight - in fact, the worst incident was when a bomb made a direct hit on a chicken house in High Street, Hampton Hill - obviously a prime military target! Two more fell on open ground off Broom Road and three in Home Park. Also one bomb and a spill of incendiaries were dropped on Mary's Terrace in London Road, Twickenham, causing a fire in the Station Yard and in some old disused cottages used for storing straw. Amazingly not one person seems to have been seriously injured, let alone killed, in this horrific attack on the Borough that night. Fortunately, of the bombs that fell that night, eleven failed to explode but were safely detonated within a week.

The final attack by conventional bombing in this phase of the War was to be on the night of the March 14. Incendiaries were dropped over a large area, commencing at Colebro Cottages on the north side of Twickenham Road and extending as far as the junction of Burtons Road with Uxbridge Road. This was probably the incident referred to cryptically in the local paper that week, when it was reported that a canister of incendiaries had fallen in the front garden of a private house in "an outer London district". Two of the bombs entered the front bedroom, but a fire guard team went into action so rapidly that the resultant fire was put out before much damage had been done. Fortunately the occupiers were at the back of the house and all escaped injury. The only damage apart from this was a haystack which was fired in Fulwell Golf Course.

So ended the Little Blitz on Twickenham by manned aircraft, but a far more dreaded and loathed "treat" was in store for the Borough within just three months - the V1 and V2 weapons.

§

Part 5

THE "REPRISAL" WEAPONS :
JUNE 1944 - JANUARY 1945

The summer of 1944 saw the beginning of the attack on England by the new German secret weapons - the V1 and V2. The "V" stood for Vergeltungswaffe - "reprisal weapons" - reprisals against the British bombings of German cities and the success of the D-Day landings in June 1944.

The V1 was a pilotless aircraft with a 1870lb (849kg) high explosive bomb warhead, a mixture of TNT and ammonium nitrate. It was aimed at its target from a launching ramp from a choice of sites in occupied northern France and later from Holland. It was automatically controlled by magnetic means. Its fuel tanks had just enough fuel to last until its destination; when the fuel ran out, the plane stalled and fell to earth exploding on impact. What most terrified people was when the rattling noise it made as it flew overhead suddenly stopped - this meant that the fuel had run out and the V1 was about to drop to earth. Those under the flightpath had just about twelve seconds to take cover before it exploded on impact with the ground. And the fact that they were pilotless meant that they could be launched day or night, in any weather condition. There was no respite against them - one could never relax as in the earlier days of the War when at least you did not expect bombing raids in daylight hours. So there was now no longer any beginning or end to the raids - life was one long alert, day and night.

The first V1 - or "buzz bomb", "flybomb" or "doodlebug" as it was nick-named - arrived over southern England on the morning of June 13th 1944. Over the subsequent months some 5,823 V1's were reported as reaching this country of which 2,242 landed in London. The Boroughs to suffer most were Croydon (141 V1's), Wandsworth (122) and Lewisham (114). Twickenham escaped comparatively lightly with only 27 landings, but seems to have suffered worse than the majority of its neighbours - Staines received only 7, Sunbury 4, Feltham 5, Heston 15, Richmond 8, Kingston 8 and Surbiton 20.

The first V1 to hit the Borough fell at 7.30am on June 18, just five days after the first one had reached England. It detonated on impact with a steel-framed dutch barn, just south of Holmesdale Road in Teddington. The barn, containing agricultural implements and straw, was entirely demolished. Fire also spread to neighbouring dwelling-houses, outbuildings and piggeries up to

110 feet from the point of impact as a result of flying straw brands. It resulted in serious damage to some ten houses and blast damage to approximately 300 houses up to a distance of some 430 yards. One person was seriously injured and twelve lightly. The same day another V1 struck just a few hundred yards away in the farm of Normansfield Hospital, a direct hit on a hay shelter; this time there was no damage.

The next day, June 19, however, was to see the worst casualties in this phase of the War. Very early in the morning there was a direct hit on numbers 77 and 79 Whitton High Street, killing a married couple. Then two more V1's fell, both harmlessly, one in Bushy Park near the NPL and the other in a reservoir south of the Upper Sunbury Road in Hampton. The fourth doodlebug to fall that day was not so merciful. It landed just before 8am on the corner of Water Lane and the Embankment at Twickenham and then seems to have bounced over a distance of some 37 feet, entering Gotham Villas, a three-storey detached house, before exploding. Six people living in Gotham Villas were killed instantly - a mother and her 7 year-old son, a 65 year old man and his daughter and an elderly married couple - and by the riverside four more were killed by the blast. Amongst those four was Frederick Hammerton (36), who was a Thames pilot waterman and worked for Tough Bros. Ltd., ship-builders, piloting craft downstream. His daughter, Freda, vividly remembers that day :

"On the Sunday night there were air raid warnings and we could hear these things (the V1's) going overhead, then the engine stopping and the explosions and we began to realise that something very nasty indeed was happening. We spent the night under the indoor Morrison in the shelter in our kitchen and my father said I wasn't to go to school but to stay in bed. My mother tried to sleep downstairs on the sofa and my father called out 'goodbye' as he rode off to work.

"Not long after that - I can't remember a bang but I suppose there must have been one, although I can remember the engine and then the cut-out and the silence - the windows fell out, the ceiling exploded down onto me in bed and I walked along the landing, over the glass and plaster, down to my mother. The front door had blown in and just missed her, but we were both safe. My mother dressed hurriedly and said she would go down to the pub (the Queen's Head, now the Barmy Arms) to telephone my father at work to say that we were safe. She thought he would have seen the "doodlebug" coming. They said that he hadn't arrived at Toughs and she thought it was strange as it is such a short ride up Strawberry Vale. My mother came home and suddenly she 'knew' what had happened. She ran out and then I 'knew' too. I flung on my clothes and ran down to the river to find my mother on her knees beside the body of my father where he lay on the shore. She was the first one to get to him. I remember when

I got there an A.R.P. man came up to us both. I vaguely remember the bricks, the dust and rubble from the block of flats which were over the boat arches (under the lawn and car park now in Water Lane). My father had the boat arch nearest to the Lane.

"My friend and her family lived in the block of flats in Water Lane. She and her mother and father were buried in the rubble and her brother Peter, who did a paper round, actually saw the bomb hit the block and saw where his family were buried, and guided the men where to dig. They were brought out safely. Others died there. Mr and Mrs Tom Lee, an old waterman and his wife (from whom my father had taken over the boat arch that summer), a pretty young girl and her father; and a mother and baby, and a little boy was also killed. This is how I recall it all - and the awful smell of dust and rubble everywhere: the muddle and the mess and the sheer misery. My father was only 36".

Then at 7.15 that evening another V1 landed directly on top of "Tudor House" at the corner of Cross Deep and Holmes Road. The Morrison shelter at the rear of the house was completely turned upside down and cut in half. In the house a mother and her infant son aged only 4 months were both killed, as were two passers-by in Cross Deep. The Pope's Grotto Public House was also demolished by the blast.

Finally on that fateful day of June 19 a sixth V1 fell in Longford Close, north of Hampton Sewage Works. A 76 year old lady was killed by the blast, but as the doodlebug had landed on open land behind the houses, little material damage was done to property. Altogether on that one fateful day 17 people had lost their lives and many more must have been seriously injured.

There was a few days' respite from the doodlebugs, then on the morning of June 29 one fell on a rubbish tip at the rear of Lincoln Avenue. Later that day another fell in a belt of trees near Stud House in Home Park and detonated in the air 30 feet above ground. Within the next two weeks two more doodlebugs fell in Bushy Park, one within the boundary of the U.S. Army "Wide Wings" Camp and the other just north-west of the Diana Fountain. In all four cases, no substantial damage was done to property, except for blast damage to windows, and there were no casualties at all.

The doodlebug that landed on Warner Brothers' Teddington studios in Broom road on the evening of July 5 was not so merciful. It fell on top, or near, a welded steel cylindrical tank containing approximately 2,000 gallons of diesel oil adjoining stage number 2. The oil scattered and ignited, setting fire to the stage, office block opposite and other adjacent buildings. The Civil Defence, ambulances and fire appliances were on the scene within minutes, but the fire-men were unable to save the large studio, which was completely gutted. The roof collapsed and, except for the four walls which remained standing, was now nothing but a mass of twisted girders. Up to that time Warner Brothers' Studios turned out some ten per cent of Britain's film production. The last completed picture at the studios was *Flight from Folly* starring Pat Kirkwood, Hugh Sinclair and Sydney Howard. The bomb interrupted this film, but it was finally completed in a garage attached to the Studios. The main stage, built on the Hollywood plan in 1936, was completely destroyed. The Ministry of Works would not allow the necessary material or labour to carry out repairs, so the studios were closed down in October 1944.

Warner Brothers' Studio, Broom Road, Teddington, after being hit by a V1 on July 5th 1944.
(Courtesy John Tasker)

Eric Bourne, a frequent visitor to the Studios in his capacity as film correspondent of the Richmond & Twickenham Times, vividly remembered that day:

"I was then living in Tennyson Avenue. I was writing a report for the

Richmond and Twickenham Times in my sitting room. It was a beautiful sunny afternoon. War could not have seemed further away. Suddenly the noise of a doodle-bug could be heard overhead. I took refuge in a cupboard under the stairs. The motor of the doodle-bug cut out. There was an ominous silence, followed by a terrific explosion which shook the house. I came out of my refuge and saw a black cloud of smoke rising in the direction of Teddington.

"With many other people I walked up the road, wondering what had been hit. Reports soon spread that it was the film studio. It was not long before I learned that my friend, "Doc" Salomon, production manager, had been killed. He was killed by a blast in his office on the ground floor of the administration block. Killed with him was an English colleague. A third man died elsewhere in the building. Incidentally for days after the bombing a multitude of dead fish collected near Richmond Bridge. They had been poisoned by the oil which flowed down the Thames".

It was only now that the general public were informed by the Government of these new German weapons unleashed on southern England - the V1s. Sir Winston Churchill, the Prime Minister, gave details in the House of Commons of casualties so far and stressed that no effort would be spared in winning the battle against this weapon. "But I am sure", he confidently asserted, "that London will never be conquered and will never fail and that her renown, triumphing over every ordeal, will long shine among men". But within a few days a great fear set in and a second great exodus from London began, with parties of children, with their mothers in many instances, leaving for the countryside. By the end of July some 7,000 women and children had been evacuated from the Borough of Twickenham. Mrs Marjorie Price, a teacher at St Mary and St Peter's School in Teddington, escorted several parties of her schoolchildren to Wales and to safety at this time of great fear.

The next three V1s to fall in the Borough all managed to avoid built-up areas. One fell south of Ellerman Avenue in Crane Park and exploded in the trees. Another fell in the grounds of Hampton Court Palace by the wall of the Broad Walk and the other in Bushy Park just behind the Greyhound Hotel at Hampton Court.

On July 21 two more V1s fell in Twickenham - the first in the front garden of 17 Talma Gardens, injuring sixteen people, the second in the Sports Ground of the Metropolitan and City Police Orphanage south of Wellesley Road, injuring twelve, two of them seriously. Wilf Kershaw, then in the Auxiliary Fire Service, was in the bath at his home in Craneford Way when the first doodle-bug came over. When it exploded in Talma Gardens it nearly blew him out of the bath!

July 24th 1944 was another black day. A flying bomb fell in the afternoon on the east side of Argyle Road, Teddington. The residents of this part of Teddington had already suffered terribly on the night of 29/30 November 1940 and now they were to suffer again. Seven houses were made completely uninhabitable, 15 more were severely damaged and blast damage affected property over a wide radius. It was estimated that over a thousand houses were damaged in some degree. Nearly the whole of Argyle Road was wiped out and many houses in Somerset Road and Church Road were condemned as unsafe structures. It brought production to a standstill at Stanley Electrical Works in Latimer Road . The firm manufactured electrical and radio components, vital for the War. There were 83 casualties altogether including nine people killed and fifteen seriously injured; of the fatalities eight lived in Argyle Road and one in Church Road. The damage to property from the November 1940 raids and from the doodlebug was so severe that this area is only just being rebuilt. Norman Longmate, in his book, *The Doodlebugs*, quotes the experiences of a soldier's wife, living in Argyle Road, who decided on this day to visit her former office at Weybridge to show off her new baby. When she arrived back at Teddington she found a police cordon across Church Road. When a policeman asked her where was going, she replied, "Home. I live at the end of Argyle Road, corner of Somerset Road". He replied, "You mean, you did". He then told her what had happened and took her to the nearest rest centre at the Baptist Church. When she went back to see her house, all she could see was a mountain of rubble.

Three days later a flying bomb fell harmlessly in one of the paddocks north of the Hampton Court Road between Hampton Wick and Hampton Court. The Borough then enjoyed a brief respite of over two weeks without an incident. Then on August 13 a V1 dropped, again harmlessly, in the tree nursery in the meadows south of Home Park opposite Thames Ditton.

Eight days later three more fell on the Borough. The first fell on the pavement at the junction of Gloucester Road, Broad Lane and Uxbridge Road in Hampton, with 23 casualties but no fatalities. The second dropped on nursery land opposite the "Shrubberies" in Buckingham Road, Hampton, and the third fell on Strawberry Hill Golf Course near the entrance opposite Walpole Gardens. Only slight damage to property was caused in the last two cases.

Two days later a V1 fell directly onto numbers 11 and 12 Seymour Gardens in Twickenham. Considerable damage was caused to 40 houses, including some in Haggard Road and Richmond Road, although street shelters at both ends of the road were undamaged. The four fatalities included a mother and her seven weeks-old baby and a young boy of only 14 months. Then four hours later there was a direct hit on the back of 6 Stanley Road, Teddington, near the junction of Hampton Road. There used to be a small terrace of shops here, including dining rooms, a newsagent and a butcher. Three shops and a small works at the rear were completely demolished and some 30 shops and terraced houses were badly damaged. Blast damage was felt over a large area and was also responsible for the collapse of the Wesleyan Methodist church opposite. A 40 year old man was also killed walking down Hampton Road.

The next day a bomb fell harmlessly in the River Thames south of Kingston Bridge and opposite the "Wilderness".

The last V1 to fall on the Borough was on August 29 in the afternoon, but was to be a deadly farewell from the enemy. It landed in the garden of the corner house at the junction of Montrose Avenue and Ryecroft Avenue in Whitton, but the blast caused at least seven houses to be made completely uninhabitable and produced extensive damage to many nearby properties. It also took the lives of four people that afternoon.

This was to be the last V1 or doodlebug to fall in the Borough during the War, although this was not quite the end of this area's sufferings. A far more awesome and terrifying weapon was to be unleashed against this country - the second of Germany's "reprisal" weapons - the V2. This was a rocket driven by liquid oxygen and alcohol. It rose to a height of some 50 miles, travelled at about 4,000 mph and had a range of some 200 miles. Its nose consisted of a one-ton high-explosive bomb. It was even more terrifying than the V1 because at least the doodlebug could be seen and heard coming and there were a few seconds to take cover if the engine cut out. There was also a chance of bringing them down with anti-aircraft fire before they reached London. With the V2 rocket there was absolutely no defence against it, besides the capture of its launching site, and there was no warning of its arrival - it literally dropped out of the sky and exploded on impact with the ground at a huge velocity.

A total of almost 1,200 V2's were aimed at London, killing some 2,724 people. Luckily for the people of West London, few V2 rockets reached this side of the capital and, in fact, only one rocket fell on this Borough. It was in the early hours of the morning of January 7th 1945 that a rocket fell on the railway embankment at the rear of 59-61 Fairfax Road, Teddington, leaving a crater some 40 feet wide and 8ft 6in deep. Fortunately there were no fatalities, but one person was seriously injured and five slightly. About 11 houses were damaged and the gasometer, about 115 yards away by the level crossing, was ignited.

§

Part 6

FINAL MONTHS

So ended the physical depredations and onslaught on the Borough, but only the beginning of years of work necessary to rebuild and repair much damaged property. While it has to be admitted that Twickenham escaped lightly compared with many parts of London, yet the damage caused cannot be underestimated. According to official Borough statistics 654 properties had to be demolished or were so damaged that they had to be pulled down. From another 762 properties the occupiers had to be evacuated before the premises could be repaired; 29,000 other properties were repaired. Forty-two historical buildings were damaged and Radnor House was entirely destroyed in 1940. Five schools were damaged and two churches had to be demolished. More important than all this, of course, was the physical loss of life - 161 according to official statistics - and 275 seriously injured. Memories of all this remain vividly with many residents to this day.

For those made homeless by the bombing, there was to be much hardship and waiting to be endured before they were rehoused. The newspapers soon reported dissatisfaction by some of the homeless in Twickenham over the treatment they had received at York House. "We want homes, not billets", was their plea. A Twickenham Residents' Protection association was quickly formed to petition the Council to speed up the repair of damaged houses. The Borough Engineer responded quickly but in a different way by putting up the first of 100 Nissen emergency huts for those who had lost their homes through bombing. By Christmas 1944 huts were being put up in Seymour Gardens, Twickenham, and at Little Queen's Road, Teddington. Further huts were to be put up in Argyle Road, Broad Street, Alpha Road and facing Fulwell Golf Course. By now, of the 462 persons requiring homes, 208 had been provided for, but still 77 families were without homes.

But all this discontentment was forgotten - albeit briefly - when the country celebrated VE Day and then the end of the War in August 1945, and everyone looked forward to a return to normality and a new era of peace.

Sources of Information

Primary sources

At the Public Record Office:
>Incident Reports (HO186/2409)
>Air raid damage (HO192/521,560,589)
>Bombs dropped by Piloted Aircraft (HO198/18-23,45)
>Flying bombs (HO198/79-93; AIR 20/4128)
>V2's (HO198/106)
>Summary of Air raids (HO198/187,191)
>Statistical records (HO198/219)
>Twickenham ARP (HO207/901-5)

At Richmond Local Studies Library:
>Register of Incidents (L940.544/LC10.464)
>War Damage Incident Book (L940.544T)
>Situation Report (L940.34)
>Air Raid Casualties admitted to Hospital (LC10.462)
>Air Raid Precautions, etc (L355.232T)
>Properties damaged by bombs (with map)(L940.544T)
>*Borough of Twickenham : Civil Defence 1939-1945 : Salute to the People's Service*, June 1945 (in L.355.232T)
>Imperial War Graves Commission - list of War Dead
>Letters from Verena Simmons of Teddington
>File on Broom Road, Teddington; Borough of Twickenham :
>Minutes of Proceedings, Vols 11-15 and Abstracts of Accounts
>*Richmond & Twickenham Times*
>*Thames Valley Times*

Secondary sources include

The Thames on Fire by LM Bates (1985)
The Encyclopaedia of 20ᵗʰ Century Warfare, ed. N. Franklin (1985)
London At War : The Hulton-Deutsch Collection, C. Hardy & N.Arthur (1989)
The London Blitz, September 1940 - May 1941, Daily Mail / Evening Standard (1990)

Continued overleaf

Secondary sources *(continued)*

A People's War, P.Lewis (1986)
The Doodlebugs, N.Longmate (1981)

Of local relevance are:

> Borough of Twickenham Local History Society papers and
> newsletters
> Kelly's Directory of Twickenham, etc. 1940
> *The Birth and Growth of Hampton Hill,* ed. M.Orton (1965)
> *TBC 90. The Story of Teddington Baptist Church,* Teddington
> Baptist Church.

Also tape-recorded interviews with Freda Hammerton, Daisy Wagstaff,
Marjorie Price, Wilf Kershaw, Henry Pease and Donald Simpson.

A fully referenced copy is deposited in the Richmond Local Studies Collection.

———————————

The Borough of Twickenham Local History Society is a member of the British Association for Local History and is affiliated to the London and Middlesex Archaeological Society and to the Arts Council of the London Borough of Richmond upon Thames. The Society was formed in April 1962 and aims to bring together people who are interested in all aspects of local history in the area which includes Twickenham, Teddington, the Hamptons, Whitton and St. Margarets.

Activities of the Society include meetings on the first Monday of each month from October to May with illustrated talks of local interest. The meetings are held in St Mary's Church Hall, Church Street, Twickenham at 8 p.m.

The Society encourages research and has published over 80 papers as well as numerous newsletter articles. Details of some recent papers are given overleaf.

Membership benefits of the Society include:

- ☐ free admittance to all lectures
- ☐ newsletters 3 times a year
- ☐ assistance with research
- ☐ outings to places of interest
- ☐ discounts on Society publications

For more information please contact:
Sheila Brook, Membership Secretary,
86 Cole Park Road, Twickenham TW1 1JA,
or view our website at
www.btlhs.co.uk.

The Borough of Twickenham Local History Society

Recent publications

Church Street Twickenham. E A Morris and T H R Cashmore. Occasional paper no 7. Published December 1999. £6

One Hundred Years of Shopping in the Old Borough of Twickenham. *The high streets of Twickenham, Teddington and the Hamptons, 1899-1999.* Paper no 79. November 1999. £4

Medieval Teddington. *The Story of a Manor of Westminster Abbey in the 14th century.* Mary F Clark. Paper no 78. October 1999. £3.50

Whitton Park and Whitton Place. P Foster and D H Simpson. Paper no 41. Revised edition July 1999. £3

Lady Frances Waldegrave, Political Hostess at Strawberry Hill 1856-1879. Kathleen Carroll. Paper no 77. April 1998. £3.50.

This is only a selection of the titles currently in print which are available from local bookshops and libraries.

For more information please contact:

Publications Committee
75 Radnor Road
Twickenham TW1 4NB.